BIG CATS

CHEETAHS

Don Middleton

The Rosen Publishing Group's
PowerKids Press™
New York

This book is dedicated to my wife Sue and my daughters Jody and Kim. Without their support, my writing and other wildlife adventures would not have been possible. Also, a special thanks to author and friend Diana Star Helmer for believing in me.

Published in 1999 by The Rosen Publishing Group, Inc.
29 East 21st Street, New York, NY 10010

First Edition

Book Design: Danielle Primiceri

Photo Credits: Cover © 1997 Digital Vision Ltd.; p. 4 © Mark Newman/International Stock; p. 6 © Ronn Maratea/International Stock; pp. 8, 16, 19, 20, 22 © 1997 Digital Vision Ltd.; p. 10 © Telegraph Colour Library 199/FPG International; p. 13 © Lee Kuhn 1991/FPG International; p. 14 © Tony Miller 1993/FPG International.

Middleton, Don.
    Cheetahs/ by Don Middleton.
        p.   cm. — (Big cats)
    Includes index.
    Summary: An introduction to the physical characteristics, habits, natural environment, and interaction with humans of the cheetah, considered to be the fastest land animal on Earth.
    ISBN 0-8239-5212-6
    1. Cheetah—Juvenile literature. [1. Cheetah.] I. Title. II. Series: Middleton, Don. Big Cats.
QL737.C23M5424 1998
599.75'9—dc21

97-48445
CIP
AC

Manufactured in the United States of America

CONTENTS

WILD CATS

Cheetahs are one of the eight **species** (SPEE-sheez) of "big cats." Long ago, cheetahs lived in Africa, Europe, Asia, and even North America. Today, they live in Africa and in very small areas in central Asia. Cheetahs live on large open grassland areas.

Unlike lions, tigers, **leopards** (LEP-erdz), and **jaguars** (JA-gwarz), cheetahs cannot roar. Also different from other big cats, cheetah babies are not called cubs. They are called kittens, just like baby house cats.

◀ The word "cheetah" comes from a word in the Hindi language that means "spotted one."

THE SPOTTED WIND

6

There are seven **subspecies** (SUB-spee-sheez) of cheetah—five live in Africa and two can be found in Asia. Asian cheetahs are a little bigger and have darker fur than their African cousins. Today, the number of cheetahs living in Asia is very small. And in some Asian countries, all of the cheetahs have been killed.

Cheetahs are about 31 inches tall. Their bodies can grow to be six feet long. A cheetah's tail can be two feet long. Cheetahs can weigh between 100 and 120 pounds. Females are usually smaller than males.

◀ Cheetahs live in over twenty countries in Africa. The country of Namibia has the largest number of these cats, with more than 4,000 living there.

A CAT WITH TWO COATS

Cheetahs are beautiful animals. Most cheetahs have yellow fur covered with black spots. All cheetahs have two black stripes running up and down their faces. **Scientists** (SY-en-tists) think these black stripes may shade their eyes from the sun when cheetahs hunt during the day. They may also help cheetahs to hide in tall grass.

There is also a rare kind of cheetah called a king cheetah. Its fur looks very different from the fur of a regular cheetah. King cheetahs have black stripes running along their bodies from front to back. Both regular and king cheetah kittens can be born in the same **litter** (LIH-ter). King cheetahs are only found in and around the African country of Zimbabwe.

The stripes down a cheetah's face are called tear marks. ▶

BUILT FOR SPEED

Cheetahs are the fastest land animals on Earth. They can reach speeds of up to 70 miles per hour for a short time. That's faster than cars are allowed to drive on most highways!

Cheetahs have long legs and their backs bend easily. This helps cheetahs take steps that are up to 22 feet long when they're running. Cheetahs have an extra large heart and big lungs too. This helps them take extra large breaths when they run fast. Their pointed toes and short claws help them get a good grip on the ground.

Cheetahs can only run at full speed for 900 feet. Then they get tired and need to rest before they can run again.

PREDATORS AND PREY

Cheetahs are smaller than lions and tigers, but they are still deadly **predators** (PRED-uh-terz). Cheetahs usually hunt small, deer-like animals such as gazelles or impalas. They like to hunt during the day. Usually they hunt alone but sometimes a few males will hunt together.

At first, a cheetah moves slowly toward its **prey** (PRAY). When it is 300 to 600 feet away, the cheetah races after the animal. Within a few seconds, the cheetah catches its prey and knocks it over with a slap of its paw. Then the cheetah kills the animal by biting its neck.

After killing a large animal, a cheetah quickly drags it to a hiding place and begins to eat. Larger predators such ▶ as lions and leopards often steal a cheetah's food.

BABY CHEETAHS

A female cheetah will **mate** (MAYT) with a male cheetah when she has no kittens to care for. After mating, the male leaves. Three to four months later, the female gives birth to as many as nine kittens. Usually a cheetah will have about four kittens.

Each newborn kitten is about half the size of a human baby. The kittens' heads and backs are covered with long gray fur. The mother cheetah carries the kittens from one hiding place to another to keep them safe from hungry predators. The kittens drink their mother's milk so they can grow strong and healthy.

◀ Cheetah kittens start to lose their gray fur when they are about three months old. It is usually gone by the time the kittens turn two years old.

15

GROWING UP

The first three months of a cheetah's life are very dangerous. The little kittens are too small to run away from lions, leopards, **hyenas** (HY-ee-nuhz), and wild dogs. Only half the litter usually survives to become adult cheetahs.

When they are three months old, cheetah kittens begin to follow their mother when she hunts. Sometimes when they try to help, the kittens make too much noise and scare away all the animals. At about eight months old, the young cheetahs start to kill their own prey. When the cheetah kittens are about eighteen months old, they leave their mother to begin their own lives.

◀ As cheetah kittens grow up, their gray kitten fur is replaced with short spotted fur.

CHEETAHS AND PEOPLE

Unlike other big cats, cheetahs hardly ever attack people. Many years ago, people even tamed cheetahs and kept them as pets. In India, one ruler had over 1,000 cheetahs. Today, people are not allowed to keep a cheetah without special permission.

People cause many problems for cheetahs. In some parts of Africa people come to watch the cheetahs while they hunt. But sometimes these people make a lot of noise and scare away the prey. Also, people called **poachers** (POH-cherz) kill cheetahs **illegally** (il-LEE-gul-lee) and sell their fur, claws, teeth, and other parts.

Even though cheetahs don't roar, they do make other sounds. They ▶ purr, growl, hiss, bark, and even make a chirping sound.

CHEETAHS IN ZOOS

For many years cheetahs in zoos got sick and died but nobody knew why. Scientists discovered that the food the cheetahs were eating wasn't good for them. The zookeepers changed the cheetahs' food. Now cheetahs in zoos can live for ten years or more. In the wild, cheetahs usually live for only three to eight years.

Today, many cheetah kittens are born in zoos. Some of these kittens may be set free in wildlife parks where they can live, hunt, and raise their own families.

◀ More than 700 cheetah kittens have been born at the De Wildt Cheetah Centre in South Africa. The Centre is helping to make sure we will always have cheetahs that we can learn about and enjoy.

A FUTURE FOR CHEETAHS

In many areas of both Africa and Asia, wild cheetahs are disappearing. The grasslands where cheetahs live are being made into farms. Farmers build fences to keep their animals from running away. These fences also keep the wild animals that cheetahs eat from getting fresh grass. These animals die and then cheetahs and other predators starve.

Some countries have made wildlife parks where cheetahs are safe. But other countries are doing very little to help cheetahs. People must learn that all animals need places where they can live safe and free.

GLOSSARY

hyena (HY-ee-nuh) A dog-like animal who eats other animals for food.

illegal (il-LEE-gul) Against the law.

jaguars (JA-gwarz) One of the four species of great cats. They live in Central and South America and have spotted coats.

leopard (LEP-erd) One of the four species of great cats. They live in Africa and Asia and have spotted coats.

litter (LIH-ter) A number of baby animals born to the same mother at the same time.

mate (MAYT) A special joining of a male and female body. After mating, the female may have a baby growing inside her body.

poacher (POH-cher) A person who kills animals that are protected by law.

predator (PRED-uh-ter) An animal that kills another animal for food.

prey (PRAY) An animal that is eaten by another animal for food.

scientist (SY-en-tist) A person who studies the way things are and act in the universe.

species (SPEE-sheez) A group of animals that are very much the same.

subspecies (SUB-spee-sheez) A group of animals that are similar but have some differences.

WEB SITES:

To learn more about cheetahs, check out this Web site:
http://www.neocomm.net/~eadams/cheetah.html

23

INDEX